Hard Rain, Hard Wind

poems by

Jamie Weaver

Finishing Line Press
Georgetown, Kentucky

Hard Rain, Hard Wind

Copyright © 2016 by Jamie Weaver
ISBN 978-1-944899-48-6 First Edition
All rights reserved under International and Pan-American Copyright Conventions.
No part of this book may be reproduced in any manner whatsoever without written permission from the publisher, except in the case of brief quotations embodied in critical articles and reviews.

ACKNOWLEDGMENTS

The author would like to thank her mother Neva for allowing her to delve into mounds of private family artifacts and make them public.

Publisher: Leah Maines

Editor: Christen Kincaid

Cover Art: Frame family photo archives

Author Photo: Tina Brannon

Cover Design: Elizabeth Maines

Printed in the USA on acid-free paper.
Order online: www.finishinglinepress.com
         also available on amazon.com

Author inquiries and mail orders:
Finishing Line Press
P. O. Box 1626
Georgetown, Kentucky 40324
U. S. A.

Table of Contents

"There is not a moment without some duty" ... 1
Get Dressed ... 2
Glad Thanksgiving Day ... 3
5:00 A.M. Again ... 4
Reverence ... 5
True Valor ... 6
418 Sugar St. ... 7
"No man was ever so much deceived by another, as by himself" ... 8
To Cabin Creek ... 9
Damp Clothes ... 10
One Nice Woman ... 11
She's Going Home to Her Husband ... 12
All in a Day's Work ... 13
Small Job ... 14
The Truck Patch ... 15
Awash ... 16
Cutting a Path ... 17
Swimming ... 18
Pressed and Mended ... 19
Hard Feelings ... 20
Anna ... 21
Blood Pressure ... 22
A Chicken Dinner and a Very Nice Time ... 23
"The falling drops at last will wear the stone" ... 24
About the Author ... 25

The family wanted Joe to be a dentist, like his father; Joe's birth name was Clyde Painless Frame, so that when it came time to hang his shingle outside his dental office, his name would also be his slogan: "C. Painless Frame for Your Dental Needs." They had high hopes, but things fell apart. Joe's father left his mother Anna for another woman, and Anna died when Joe was five. Joe was raised by his grandmother Lou and grew up poor in rural Appalachia; he became a farmer, a veteran, a boilermaker, and a drinker.

These poems are for my grandfather Joe.

"There is not a moment without some duty"

Nice day, I butchered a hog and
Ground the sausage and lard, put up 65 quarts
Busy day, I went to a basketball game and
Dried clothes inside for the first time this season
Cloudy day, I pressed some trousers and
Baked a berry cobbler for supper
Cold day, I rode the mare home from Mr. McNeal's and
Went to Wellsville to get my shoes soled
Glad day, I didn't go to school and
December 25th brought us all something we enjoyed
Warm day, I husked corn at the barn and
Stayed up until after twelve last night
Foggy day, I was busy all forenoon in school and
Mended my overcoat tonight

Get Dressed

Come out in the shade
    I finished bringing in the wheat
        and things look so fresh after the rain
Come out and stay for supper
    I picked a bushel of beans
        and I need some real comfort
Come out on the porch
    I painted and cleaned the kitchen
        and school doesn't start until Tuesday
Come out and be my first
    I had a shower
        and they have gone to town

Glad Thanksgiving Day

Come in for a bit, the east wind is blowing
        we have rabbit for dinner and
        a lecture on the phonograph

Let's not do much, dear, but rest by the furnace
        news of the war is raging, but
        we are the children of kings

5:00 A.M. Again

Celebrated my birthday canning peaches all alone
Worked some crab apples and made some boneset tea

> We had a terrible electric storm
> Lightning struck the barn
> Damage was done
> Still got up to milk and feed the hogs

Earthquakes and fog don't last
But the sun comes up every day

Reverence

Left this morning
        for God knows where
        in the service of my country
So lonesome and blue
        only God knows how I hate this place

I miss home so much
        the first frost,
                everything white in the morning
                the fog clearing
        clothes drying on the line
        the last tomatoes from the garden

True Valor

A sultry morning, so hot
      in a bad hot country, killing
      the living we can do without
Day after day
      we are ready, loaded, cool
      amid the sulphur, the sun, the spinning
Too tired for a good conscience

418 Sugar St.

I can't sleep, so I'm up writing
        I do hate to see you go
                my heart aches and I'm alone

I wish I could
        meet you tonight at Baltimore
                in your pretty clothes
        lie down together
        while away the gloom

"No man was ever so much deceived by another, as by himself"

I got quite a bit of living yet to do
A storm seems to be coming
        and I've been almost dead
        all this time, unaware

To Cabin Creek

Found a sedan I think will do
      for a ride down to home country
Meet me on Erie Street
      ready to leave tomorrow
We'll have waffles for supper and
      drink at lunch
Eat well and sleep well
      on these warm nights in June

Damp Clothes

A quiet morning
A bad night's sleep
I'm alone and not well
Last evening sure was grand
But a hard wind and a bad cold
Keep me close to the fire

One Nice Woman

Little "hoopy" in the heavy class
I have my doubts
She's given boys up (of course there are men left)
I'm not going to get serious
Little homely bashful windbag
Lots of things have happened in 4 years
She's mopping the floor with blue jeans and plaid shirt on
I believe I'm bored

She's Going Home to Her Husband

        I've not been asleep all night
        I was home yesterday to see her leaving
                she's 'taken our chickens to market'
        I didn't do much to stop her
        I think I'll feel better
                once I fix the well and jump in

All in a Day's Work

I cleaned the cupboards
Washed dishes
        and peeled apples
Spike has been poisoned
        I mended some
Washed a bit
        and pressed some things
Spike died last night and I buried him
I picked beans this forenoon
Washed my hair
        and went to work

Small Job

I really done a number this time
    oh boy, was I busy

This morning's gone to hell,
    and this afternoon's pretty well shot

But I still have a few more days to kill,
    a bit more property,
    and most of my cool

The Truck Patch

Flossie's calf was two days old
      the day the finches came
I planted a few potatoes
      churned nine pounds of butter
      on that warm and windy morning
The boys made ice cream in the cellar that day
      cut grass and brought in the hay
Hot weather for busy work
      nice moon for sleep

Awash

Nice morning, but hot
    took a bath
    and went down the creek
To get some honey
Rode the horse to the old home place
    it's nice and quiet at the river this evening
    went fishing with Paul, on leave from the Navy
Met some of his folks
    washed a few things
    and it rained this evening with our clothes on the line

Cutting a Path

Went to town this morning to get a job
    washed my hair and took a bath, too
        Looks as though the war ended
        They sure are celebrating in this town
        So much noise you can hardly stand it
        Most of our boys will be spared
Ended up down in the park
    got lunch and came home sad
I must keep on living
    and doing the best I can to get along

Swimming

Last night we cooked a groundhog
This afternoon I got up, head swimming with beer
Took a tumble down the steps
But I'm on the mend, on the beer again, swimming

Pressed and Mended

I've been under the weather for quite a bit
        in a furnished room somewhere
So foggy, dark, cold
        the day slipped away from me
Only God knows what I've suffered
It's beginning to snow now
        and the ground is almost covered

Hard Feelings

Couldn't get myself together long
        enough to write
Would like to come down but can't
        considering I'm still drinking
I slowed up before and quit
        and started drinking more than ever
Like the weather, you never know what
        tomorrow's going to be
Funny about the truth,
        no one's that lucky
I'd come down, but I'd get pinched
        before I got started
I expect I better shut up
        and destroy this letter
I'm half crazy and half asleep
        so that accounts for it all

Anna

She will soon have her day in the garden
                          a morning of praise, of living
              to bring back a world
              of warm washed dresses
              afternoon rains
                cherry pie and bath soap
       but only until I wake

Blood Pressure

I'm sick of my appearance
        two buttonholes in paper
            scrubbed dry
        deep plow lines in the field
Electric man
        with bad wiring

A Chicken Dinner and a Very Nice Time

I ran away from you
And stayed overnight in town,
      too chicken to come home for dinner
I'm on the wagon, but spitting blood
Doctor thinks I'm much improved,
      enough for a cutting-down and a
      working-over from you

"The falling drops at last will wear the stone"

                    I'm so sick of this drinking
                    I don't know what to do
Time slipped away this morning
Looks like I finished another one
                          in bed reading the paper
Seventy-five years I've been here
                          in the well, with everything burning up

Weaver grew up in rural West Virginia, and finds herself deeply inspired by the complex geography, history, and culture of Appalachia. Her writing and artist books explore her Appalachian experiences by embracing, questioning, and sometimes subverting the traditional folk stories, beliefs, and practices in which her childhood was steeped. Although too often dismissed as cultural outliers, Appalachians enjoy a rich history of multicultural influences and an ardent interconnectedness with the land. As a child of Appalachia, Weaver sympathizes with the fierce independence and proud reticence of her ancestors, but also believes it is the duty of all societies to question their myths and motivations. She writes new stories and retells old ones, participates in folk rituals, and wanders her native landscape, seeking to legitimize her Appalachian experiences by forcing hard truths to the surface and offering them simply as relics of the human experience, as variations of the myths and motivations that are common to us all.

In order to better understand her Appalachian upbringing and to form stronger connections between her family history and current identity as a writer, book artist, and feminist, Weaver developed *Hard Rain, Hard Wind*, in which a powerful dialogue about familial shame and reconciliation emerges between the poet, her grandfather Joe, and several generations of female family members who suffered through Joe's drinking. *Hard Rain, Hard Wind* is an exercise in reconciliation and acceptance by using lived experiences to reconstruct reality. As a female family member channeling Joe's voice, Weaver portrays him as a character deserving of empathy and uses her newfound understanding of him as a method of emotional empowerment for herself and to reclaim that power on behalf of her female ancestors.

www.ingramcontent.com/pod-product-compliance
Lightning Source LLC
Chambersburg PA
CBHW060226050426
42446CB00013B/3198